# Jack The Rippe

## A Musical Play

Book and Lyrics by
Ron Pember
and
Denis de Marne

Music by
Ron Pember

Samuel French - London
New York - Toronto - Hollywood

# JACK THE RIPPER

A Musical Reconstruction of incidents relating to the East End murders which took place between Friday, August 31st and Friday, November 9th, 1888, set in a Music Hall and the surrounding streets, as performed by the Inhabitants of Whitechapel

First presented at the Players' Theatre, London, on June 25th, 1974

Subsequently presented by Larry Parnes (by arrangement with the Players' Theatre) in association with Brian Rix and Ray Cooney at the Ambassadors Theatre, London, on September 17th, 1974, with the following cast of characters

| | |
|---|---|
| Marie Kelly/Music Hall Soubrette | Terese Stevens |
| Lizzie Stride/Queen Victoria | Eleanor McCready |
| Annie Chapman | Elaine Holland |
| Polly Anne Nicholls | Linda Rusby |
| Liza Pearl | Bernice Adams |
| Martha Tabram | Christine Edmonds |
| Catherine Eddowes | Sandra Holloway |
| Frances Coles | Helena Shenel |
| Montague Druitt | Howard Southern |
| Chairman | Peter Spraggon |
| Daniel Mendoza | Roy Stone |
| Dinky Nine-Eights ⎫ | Jonty Miller |
| Bluenose Stack ⎬ his gang | Derek Connell |
| Slop Wallace ⎭ | Jack Chissick |
| Lord Overcoat | Gerald Taylor |
| Police Sergeant Coles | Charles West |
| Policeman, etc. | Harry Goodier |
| | John Denton |
| | Graham Richards |
| | Alan C. Turvey |

The play directed, and the settings by, REGINALD WOOLLEY

NOTE: The characters of the show are called upon to play more than one role. It is essential that this is adhered to as it is an integral part of the format of the show as a whole. They have a life within the Music Hall and also in reality

**The Chairman,** representing authority as he does, also plays the authoritative roles of Sir Charles Warren, the Magistrate and the Docks Foreman

**Montague Druitt** is known also as Toynbee by the locals. Toynbee Hall is his place of employment. He also plays the villain in the melodrama, and the magician

# MUSICAL NUMBERS

## ACT I

| | |
|---|---|
| *Saturday Night* | Polly and the Company |
| *Sing Sing* | The Company |
| *Generally Nice* | Marie |
| *God Bless Us* | The Company |
| *Good-bye Day* | Marie and the Girls |
| *What A Life* | The Gang and the Girls |
| *Love* | Marie |
| *Ripper's Going To Get You* | Annie and the Gang |

## ACT II

| | |
|---|---|
| *God Bless* (reprise) | The Company |
| *Charlie And Queenie* | Lizzie and the Chairman |
| *Half A Dozen Pints* | Marie |
| *There's A Boat Coming In* | The Company |
| *There Ain't Any Work Today* | Chairman and the Company |
| *Look At Them* | The Company |
| *Suspects* | Martha and the Gang |
| *Policemen's Chorus* | Police Sergeant Coles and Constables |
| *Step Across The River* | Marie and Lizzie |
| *Montage* | The Company |
| *Saturday Night* (reprise) | The Company |

The Music for this play can be obtained from Samuel French Ltd

# NOTE ON THE SETTING

The forestage area represents a Victorian Music Hall, with tables, chairs, and a table for the Chairman. Where possible this should be extended into the auditorium in order to link the Audience closely with the Music Hall scenes. Upstage of this is a raised area framed with a false proscenium decorated with lights, which are brought up when a Music Act is being performed. The area beyond represents the "real" streets of Whitechapel.

# ACT I

## OVERTURE

*"The Steampacket", Flower and Dean Street, Whitechapel. A Saturday night in autumn, 1888*

*The set is an open stage. In the foreground are some tables and chairs. Higher levels on each side give the impression of theatre boxes in a crude form of early Music Hall. The acting area represents the streets of White-chapel of the stage of the Steam Packet Music Hall. (See plan on p. 49 and Note on p. vii)*

*The crowds begin to stream into the streets to the Music Hall. The Chairman waits to greet people at the door. A tart (Polly) stands under a light in the street. She speaks to a Man as he passes by*

**Polly** Oi, mate, fancy having a good time?

*The Man passes on*

*Another man approaches*

Come on, Johnny, have a bit of fun, it'll make you forget your troubles.

*A Salvationist walks by*

Here you are, sonny, wanna buy a gargle for a nice girl? Go on, you miserable sod, I hope you catch a dose.

*A shadow looms large on the back wall. The shape is of a man dressed in a cloak, carrying a Gladstone bag and wearing a top hat. Polly addresses the figure in the shadows*

Hello, Jack. I must say we don't often see such a nice gent as you around these parts. Fancy giving a girl a good time? Just back from the New World, are you? (*As the shadow grows larger*) Come on, enjoy yourself, have a good time, it's Bank Holiday, isn't it? It's *Saturday*, isn't it?

*The shadow looms even larger and the music reaches a climax—a shaft of light cuts across the stage as Dan Mendoza and his boys, Slop, Dinky and Bluenose, are thrown out of the Pub*

**Dan** (*calling back*) All right, Fitzy, all right, mate, we've got long memories we have. I'll have you for this one of these days.
**Bluenose** Bleeding sauce, ain't it?
**Dinky** Just 'cos we couldn't pay.
**Dan** Hey, Slop, how much you got?
**Slop** Nothing, Dan.
**Dan** You wouldn't be lying to me, now would you?

**Slop** Aw, Dan, would I lie to you? I wouldn't, would I?
**Dan** You just try, that's all. Oi, Polly. What have you got?
**Polly** The pox. Want it?
**Dan** I'm talking about money, ain't I, I'm borasic.
**Polly** I ain't got any money, have I? I wouldn't be standing out here if I had, would I?

*Other people begin to fill the street, greeting each other—a build-up of natural sounds; baby crying, spoons, arguing, etc*

**Dan** Oi, Overcoat, lend us a few bob, will you?
**Lord Overcoat** (*pushing a barrow*) I want to be fair to you, Dan boy, but also most of all, I must be fair to me. If I lend you a few bob—where's me profits?
**Busker** On a float, on a boat, we will float, up and down the Mississippi . . .

*A Religious Fanatic, carrying a banner, pushes his way forward*

**Salvationist** Abandon hope, all ye Heathens. Prepare to be consumed by the fires of thine own destruction for the day of retribution is at hand.
**Polly** Come on, mate, you want to have a good time, don't you? It's Bank Holiday, ain't it? It's Saturday, ain't it? (*She sings*)

"SATURDAY NIGHT"                    No. 1

    Oh delight
    Saturday night
    All bleeding week you've been hiding.
    Now you're here
    Clouds disappear
    Gawd how the sun is shining
**All** Gawd how the sun is shining!

    Oh delight
    Saturday night
    Oh how I wanted to kiss yer
    Safe from harm
    Locked in your arms
    You'll never know how I've missed yer.

    Sunday we sleep a lot
    Monday night is best forgot
    Tuesday night we never knew how to handle you
    Wednesday you're a bore
    Thursday night's a bleeding whore
    Friday night could never hold a candle to you.

    But oh delight
    Saturday night
    Now you've come back it'll cost you
    How I cried

I nearly died
I really thought I'd lost you.

*The music keeps going underneath while over the top the Girls shout to one another*

**Annie** 'Ere, Liz, save us a bed for later, will yer?

**Liz** You get your fourpence, gel, I'll fix you up.

**Marie** (*indicating the Salvationist*) Here, Polly, who's that?

**Polly** That's that psalm-singing-do-gooder, Mr Druitt from Toynbee Hall.

**Marie** Here, Druitt. Put your bible down, son, and get hold of this! (*She sings*)
  Sunday's me day of rest
  Monday night I'm too depressed
  Tuesday night I never felt very willing.
  Wednesday it's half the price
  Thursday if you're very nice
  Friday you can have us twice for just one shilling.

**All** Oh delight
  Saturday night
  Much as I love you, yer grieve me
  You break my heart
  Whenever we part
  So please say you'll never leave me.

**Salvationist** Abandon hope, all ye Heathens. Prepare to be consumed by the fires of thine own destruction for the day of retribution is at hand.

**Chairman** (*adopting the character of the Salvationist*) Abandon hope, all ye heathens, the day of retribution is at hand. Cast aside your wicked ways. Cast aside all hopes of heaven.

**Dan** Where's heaven, mate, somewhere up the Mile End Road?

**Chairman** Mend your ways, you sinners, or Satan will swallow you whole. He's lurking in every shadow of every street, feeding on the blood and body of every living soul.

**Dan** Well, he's lucky, we ain't had nothing to eat for a week.

**Chairman** You fool, can't you see the Angel of Death stands behind you?

**Dan** Well, it's about time he bought a round, then.

**Chairman** You are destined to sink further and further into the abyss. You are Satan's servant, drunk with wine and fornication.

**Dan** Not yet, but the night is still young.

**Chairman** Damn you all. Let the Devil come and tear your black hearts from your heathen bodies.

**Dan** The Devil's too late, the Rent Man called this morning.

**Chairman** It's not too late. It's never too late . . . (*He sings*)

"SING, SING"

**No. 2**

  Sing, sing, and let the evening ring
  With the voices of the brave

**All**  Cor blimey
Sing, sing, and let the evening ring
With the voices of the saved!
**Chairman**  Meet Brother Paul
God gave him a special gift
He has suffered with you all
Used to be a flannel thief
Yet mercifully
Saw the error of his ways
Turned his back on Lucifer
Joyfully we sing his praise.
**Dan**  Meet Charlie Small
Never went to Sunday school
Never ever said his prayers
Only in the snooker hall
He's not too bright
Never learned to read and write
It'll be a flippin miracle
If you get him to see the light.

**All**
Alleluia let the evening ring
With the many, many voices, voices of the brave.
Alleluia let the evening ring
With voices of the saved.

Sing, sing and let the evening ring
With the voices of the brave
Sing, sing let the evening ring
With the voices of the saved.

**Chairman**  Here's Liza Pearl
Once a sinner now a saint
Led a wicked lustful life
Covered up her face with paint
How high the price
To sow upon a barren bed
Threw away her wicked life
Found everlasting peace instead.
**Dan**  Here's Freddie Priest
She's the beauty, he's the beast
What a face he's lumbered with
Uglier than Aldgate East.
When he's about
Better get your finger out
Cut you up for half a crown
That's the sort of bloke he is.
**All**  *Chorus (as above)*
**Chairman**  Meet Toynbee Hall
A truly handsome gentleman
Gave up a life of luxury

To come down here to help you all
But, in return
Received the thing we all long for!
The everlasting love of God
So bountiful for evermore.

(*Speaking*) Come along, Mr Druitt, give them a bit of your fancy Speech making.

**Druitt** Good soldiers of our Lord, fellow workers together in the name of God, join with me in one united prayer, call upon the Almighty to have mercy upon these, thy forgotten children.

**Dan** Who's forgotten?

**Druitt** Brother, hearken unto me. Death and damnation is not Christianity. Christianity is LOVE, and this love shines through, even the eyes of these, our sisters-of-the-night, the poor unfortunates of Whitechapel.

**Francis Coles** I'll tell you something for nothing, mate! Your boots is a lot brighter than your head. There's not much of yer, and what there is is mostly clothes. All you ever speak is words and they're all Greek to me —so why don't you piss off!

**Druitt** May God forgive you! Join us now, Brothers, Soldiers of the Cross, workers to the greater glory in the name of our Lord Jesus Christ . . .

**Girls** Oh what a crowd
Don't we do the Army proud?
Fearless in the face of God
Faithful to the love we vowed

**Boys** Oh what a crowd
Don't we do old England proud?
Right old bunch of layabouts
Do so little, talk too loud.

**All**
Alleluia let the evening ring
With the many, many voices, voices of the brave
Alleluia let the evening ring
With the voices of the saved

Sing, sing and let the evening ring
With the voices of the brave
Sing, sing and let the evening ring
With the voices of the saved.

*During the song the Company march into the Music Hall, leaving the Boys, Marie and Annie in the street*

**Dan** Oi, Dinky, go and get Marie over here.

**Dinky** Oi, Slaggy—here.

**Marie** Who are you calling slaggy?

**Dinky** You. Here.

**Marie** Now look, why don't you go and whistle up somebody else's backyard? Can't you see I'm busy?

**Dan** (*going over to her*) Now listen, girl, any more of your lip and I'll give you one.

**Marie** Oh yeah? You lay one finger on me, cock, and I'll knock you the other side of Berner Street, as big as you are.

**Dan** Yeah?

**Marie** Yeah!

**Bluenose** Yeah?

**Dan** (*swiping him*) Who asked you to stick your blue nose in? All right, Marie, love, there's no need to get your rag up.

**Marie** Well . . . What do you want?

**Dan** We—ll, er . . .

**Marie** Oh. You ain't got any readys, have you?

**Dan** Emm—I am feeling the pinch a bit. Still I'll be all right when the boat comes in.

**Marie** I've known you a long time, haven't I, Dan?

**Dan** We were kids together, Marie.

**Marie** Yeah. We always mucked in with whatever we had, didn't we?

**Dan** I looked after you and you looked after me.

**Marie** That's right. So. I'll tell you what I'll give you.

**Dan** What, Marie?

**Marie** Nothing, mate. Not a sausage, so bugger off!

**Dan** You mingy cow. (*He lashes angrily at the Boys*) Annie—come here.

**Marie** Don't you give him anything, Annie.

**Dan** Who asked you to put your spoke in.

**Marie** You want to pick on someone your own size.

**Annie** Watcha want?

**Dan** You know what I want, don't come the old acid. How much you got?

**Annie** I haven't got nothing, have I? I mean, I wouldn't be out on the streets if I did, would I?

**Dan** Now listen, you've given me nothing for weeks, girl. If you want me to look after you, you're going to have to pay for my services the same as all the others.

**Annie** Have a heart, Dan. Times is hard, but I'll see you all right when the boat comes in.

**Dan** When the boat comes in—when the boat comes in—we'll all be dead by then. Come on, cough up, there's a limit to my generosity.

**Bluenose** If you don't cough up, I'll knock your teeth out.

**Dan** (*grabbing Bluenose*) Shut up, I swear I'll swing for you one of these days, Bluenose! Give us your bag. (*He takes Annie's bag*) You lying cow, you've got fourpence in here.

**Annie** But that's the price of my bed, Dan, if I ain't got that I'll have to sleep in the alley.

**Dan** Never mind—it's cleaner than a bed in Long Lizzie's any day.

**Marie** I told you not to give him anything, didn't I?

**Annie** I never. He just took it.

**Marie** Well, kick him in the cobblers and he won't do it twice.

**Dan** Neither would she.

**Marie** You rotten sod, give her back her money.

**Dan** What's it to do with you? She's done me a favour. I'll do her a favour, someday.

**Marie** The only favour you could do us, Mendoza, is to take a running
jump off Southwark Bridge.

*The Boys laugh at this remark*

**Dan** (*to the Boys, lashing out*) What are you laughing at? All right, Marie,
you'll be sorry for this. Bloody-well think you're a lady, don't you—I
bet you ain't even got any drawers on.

*The Boys try to look up her skirt*

**Marie** Take your hands off me. You dirty rotten, lousy, stinking, filthy
son of a double-eyed . . .

*At the height of her cursing all the Music Hall Lights snap on. Marie is now
a sweet soubrette singing a parody of an innocent ballad of the day. This
must make an impact—it is the first time the Music Hall Lights have been
used in this way*

"GENERALLY NICE"

No.
3

(*singing*) I'm the girl you all know
    Who's generally nice
    Tho' generally wouldn't look at twice
    I'm simple. Shy. Secure.
    Very quiet, rather pure
    And tho' I might seem generally tough
    I'm quite demure.

    Just an ordinary lady
    With ordinary ways
    With a clean, a very ordinary mind
    I'm shy, uncomplicated
    All as previously stated
    Unaffected by the ravages of time.

**All** She's the girl we all know
    Who's generally nice
    Tho' generally wouldn't look at twice
    And when others have betrayed
    And other lovers they have strayed
    Our girl's got the kind of looks
    That never fade.
**Marie** I'll admit when you see me
    I looks a little plain
    But I'm quiet and demure but divine
**All** There's not another lady like her
    In the whole wide world
    But I'm proud to say she's mine
**Marie** Yes I'm proud to say I'm thine
**All** Oh I'm proud to say she's mine
    All—mine.
**Chairman** Your own, your very own Marie Kelly. Welcome, ladies and

gentlemen, to the Steampacket Music Hall. How nice to see so many
friends here this evening, some old, some new. Some very new and some
very *old*. Tonight, ladies and gentlemen, we have for you a never-to-be-
forgotten night. It is not often, nay seldom, nay NEVER—no *never* has
the Steampacket had such an abundance of talent assembled for your
entertainment. Scenes of Laughter; Beauty; Grace; High Drama;
Ethereal Love; Murder; Terror—TERROR GALORE
**Frances Coles** Holy Jesus, save us all!
**Chairman** Are we downhearted?
**All** NO!
**Chairman** Then, are we all *happy*?
**All** YES!
**A Man** But we're all broke.
**All** BOOOOO!
**Chairman** Never mind, Charlie'll let us have it on the slate.
**All** Hurrah!
**A Man** But we haven't got any work.
**Chairman** Never mind. We'll be all right when the boat comes in. Now,
ladies and gentlemen—a little solemnity. I must ask you to raise your
glasses and be upstanding. To drink a loyal toast to our much-beloved
and kind-hearted—QUEEN VICTORIA. God bless her!
**All** God bless her.
**Chairman** But chiefly, your own and very dear selves. God bless you!

"GOD BLESS US"                              No.
                                                                      4

**All** God bless us. (*Singing*)
    God bless us
    Down here no-one stands alone
    And anything of yours is mine
    And what is mine's
    Me own.
**Chairman** God bless our glorious queen
    And may she reign forever more
    A finer lady never lived
    Of this I am quite sure
    She thinks of us
    She prays for us
    And hope that we may thrive
**All** But grub and work and houses
    I'm afraid she can't provide.
    God bless us

    Down here no-one stands alone
    Anything of yours is mine
    And what is mine's
    Me own. How's your father? All right!
**A Man** God bless our Lizzie Stride

She's known as Queen to all her friends
Says she comes from royalty
**Martha** Or so she still pretends
Reckons she's a princess                    **All** Yeah
With every right to reign                   **All** Oh Gawd
**Dan** If she's got royal blood in her
Then I'm the Queen of Spain
**All** I'm the Queen of ...

God bless us
Down here no-one stands alone
Anything of yours is mine
And what is mine's
Me own. How's yer father? All right!
**Lizzie** God bless Lord Overcoat
The Banana King of Poplar Green
Please keep his prices down
And his rotten apples clean
He's got to make a living
But it shall come to pass
That if I catch him diddling me
I'll kick him up the ...
**All** God bless us
Down here no-one stands alone
Anything of yours is mine
And what is mine's
Me own
Sing, sing, and let the evening ring ...
**Cathy** God bless old Toynbee Hall
He tries so hard to save us all
**A Man** Why he bothers puzzles me
It's all a load of bull
**All** Yeah, how's that.
**Druitt** I say each day we're sinking
Into a pit of sin
**Dan** Well if this is hell
Then roll on death
I hope they let me in.
**All** In, in!
All through the night
When the dark clouds are blowing
We'll be there to guide you all
And we'll never, never—never never, never, never, fail.

God bless us
Down here no-one stands alone
Anything of yours is mine
And what is mine's
Me own

Anything of yours is mine
And what is mine, what is mine—'s
Me own, me own—me own.

*As the song ends, the Lights fade into a dim street scene. It is misty. Polly
is standing under a gas lamp. We see the familiar silhouette of the cloak,
hat and Gladstone bag that we saw in the opening scene. Polly speaks
towards the direction from which the unseen figure seems to be coming. As
she speaks, the shadow comes nearer and nearer*

**Polly** Hello, Jack. Just back from the New World, are you? How about
buying a girl a nice drink? You look a respectable sort of bloke. Go
on, let your hair down. It's August Bank Holiday, isn't it? Have yourself a bit of fun, you deserve it. That's it. Come on, Jack, you come with
me, I'll show you a good time.

**No.**
**4a**

*All the while the shadow has got nearer, and at this moment he strikes.
He draws a knife across her throat. She screams. The music stops. The
crowd in the Music Hall abruptly stop and take notice. Then with a flourish
the knife turns into a bunch of flowers and we are in a Music Hall Act with
a Magician and his Assistant performing a number of tricks that always look
a little dangerous but end in safety. The Chairman speaks as a large disap-
pearing cabinet is wheeled on*

**Chairman** And now, ladies and gentlemen, Marvel the Mystic will attempt
to recreate for you that famous illusion first performed by Piraceneti in
eighteen fifty-five. Mystic's pretty young assistant, Miss Polly. Give us
a smile, Miss Polly. Miss Polly will be despatched into the streets of
Whitechapel.

*Polly does, in fact, leave*

Miss Polly Ann is at liberty to take refuge where she will among the
labyrinth of alleys and passageways of the Great Metropolis. Meanwhile, ladies and gentlemen, Marvel the Mystic will demonstrate for
you that his cabinet is completely empty and impenetrable to mere
mortals such as you or I.

*The Magician demonstrates that the cabinet is empty*

Now, ladies and gentlemen, we crave your indulgence while Mystic
summons up the supreme energy which is at his disposal and with a
flourish that will amaze you, produce from his Caligari Cabinet your
own—YOUR VERY OWN—MISS POLLY ANN NICHOLS!

*At this point, the cabinet door is flung open and from the box slumps the
dead and bloody body of Polly. Silence—then pandemonium breaks out.
The Chairman calls for and obtains silence*

A monologue to Mary Ann Nichols.
Known to her friends as Polly.

Polly Ann Nichols was an Aldgate whore
Not too pretty as I recall
Five front teeth missing from the lower jaw
Souvenir of a bar-room brawl.

She left Ireland's green lands for London
For the call of the bright city's lights
Now she's lying alone on cold mortuary stone
Not one of the prettiest sights.

She was born in the County of Derry
In a home full of trouble and strife
And Polly Ann ran away.
In the hope that one day
She would get something more out of life.

There follows a trail of disaster
That's enough to make each of us shriek
Of a baby still-born, of a body well worn
With disease of which none of us speak.

The rest is now ancient history
A story you've often heard tell
She was battered and bruised
Depraved and abused
Consumed by the fires of Hell.

Untrustful, and filthy and wicked,
And went with strange men every night,
She was lustful, and shameful and evil
So let us all say "Serves you right".

She made her own bed,
Let her lie on it.
Why should we hang our heads down in shame?
It was just circumstance
Never gave her chance
So why should we share any blame?

So let us not linger upon it
Let us all fill our glasses and sing
Let us all warm ourselves by the fire
Let us all close our ears to such things.

And so ends the story of Polly
But there's one last thing I must say
That this toothless old hag

Lying dead on a slab,
Was just fifteen years old today.

*There is a moment's silence, then the voice of Annie Chapman is heard singing tipsily in the Music Hall audience*

**Annie** (*singing*) It was only a violet, plucked for her mother's grave . . .
**Voice** Why can't you keep quiet, we're trying to get pissed over here.
**Annie** Liz—Lizzie.
**Lizzie** (*from above*) Hello, dearie.
**Annie** Have you got a room, Liz, can you do me a bed for the night?
**Lizzie** 'Course I could, dear, if you've got the readys.
**Annie** Well I did have, but Mendoza took it from me, Liz. It's getting late and I don't want to spend another night in Itchy Park.
**Lizzie** Sorry, luvvy, but if I let you in then I'd have to do the same for everybody else, and then where would I be, eh?
**Annie** You know me, Liz, I'd never let you down. I'll pay you back tomorrow, I swear I will. I'll give you a whole tanner.
**Lizzie** If you promised me a shilling, dear, the answer would still be no.
**Annie** Well, you'll be sorry. You won't get a minute's peace for the rest of your natural, if I'm found with me throat cut.
**Lizzie** They don't half fill your head with rubbish, you don't want to waste your time listening to that Sally-Ann crowd.
**Annie** It ain't safe with all these murders about.
**Lizzie** Gawd bless you, you don't want to worry your head about that, there's always been murders round here. I've seen things that would make your hair curl. When I lived up in Newington there was a woman there who was cut up in little pieces and scattered all over Haggerston Park.
**Annie** Don't, Liz, you'll give me nightmares.
**Lizzie** Life is full of little surprises.
**Annie** Go on, Liz—just one night—I'll never bother you again.
**Lizzie** Sorry, dear, if you ain't got the fourpence—you can't have a doss. You know the rules.
**Marie** Here, Annie, you want to borrow me new hat?
**Annie** Ooo yeah. Ta, Marie.
**Marie** Here you are, catch. (*She throws Annie her hat*)
**Annie** (*putting it on*) Oh yeah! I'll soon get meself another fourpence wearing this. Ta-ta!
**Marie** If you breaks me feather—I'll break your bleeding neck!
**Annie** (*going*) There'll be no messing about tonight. It ain't going to be no lay-down job, just a quick knee-trembler.
**Lizzie** (*singing*) Come back here you can have a bed

"GOOD-BYE DAY"                                    No.
                                                 5

If you earn a tanner
Or get a place at the Mile End waste
Carrying the banner

**Annie** Good-bye, day
Good-bye, day
Day is too long and too bright
I prefer night
**Marie** Don't be long with me nice new hat
And don't you break the feather
Keep your face from the alleyways
And don't go near the river.

Good-bye, day. Good-bye, day.
Take the pain
I thought you'd last forever
Let the darkness cover me
Let me hear the lullaby
That only the night can bring

Good-bye, day. Good-bye, day.
Take your grey
City smoke and fervour
Take the dull and dusty light
And let me hear the lullaby
That only the night can sing

Days are only for laughing
For music, for singers and their song.
For lovers confused by the brightness
Consider they are one
The sun is only existing
To touch them, and shower them with light
But for me days are simply too long
I prefer night
**Marie** Good-bye, day. \*Good-bye, day.    \***Annie & Lizzie** Day is too long
Take your grey\*                                              Too bright I prefer night.
City smoke and fervour
Let the dull and dusty light
And let me hear the lullaby          \***Lizzie & Annie** Take the dull
That only the night can sing              and dusty light.
**Lizzie** Keep your face from the alleyways
**Marie** Good-bye, day.
**Lizzie** Keep to the lanes where the lamps are lit
**Marie** It can't last forever.

*A pause*


*In the silence Druitt enters*


**Cathy** Hello, dearie, can I do anything for you?
**Druitt** I wonder if any of you can help me? I'm looking for a girl.
**Marie** Well—you've come to the right place then, ain't yer?

**Druitt** No. You misunderstand me. This is someone in particular I'm looking for.

**Martha** Well, I don't mind having a go.

**Marie** Look, mate, if it's something special you want, I ain't fussy—but
it'll cost yer!

**Druitt** How much?

**Marie** Are you serious?

**Druitt** Deadly. How much?

**Marie** To you—a tanner.

**Druitt** Here you are then. (*He hands her a coin*)

**Marie** Ta. Come on then, we're not doing it here, are we?

**Druitt** We're not doing anything anywhere. You wanted sixpence—you
got it.

**Marie** (*suspiciously*) I know your game, mate, I ain't taking no tanner for
nothing.

**Druitt** It's not for nothing, I can have sixpennyworth of your time, can't
I?

**Marie** (*thinking about it*) Right'o. Watcher want?

**Druitt** I'm looking for a girl who used to live in the Westminster area, but
left, and, I believe that she's now living somewhere around here.

**Marie** No—I've never seen *no lady* living down here.

**Druitt** She wasn't exactly a lady.

**Lizzie** You should know, Marie, you used to live up west, didn't you?

**Marie** Shut your mouth, Liz.

**Lizzie** Well, I couldn't tell a lie, could I, dear?

**Marie** No, I don't know anybody like that—what was her name?

**Druitt** It was Jeannette. Could be anything now, could even be—Marie.
Well—nothing to say?

**Marie** Yes, you've had your tannersworth.

**Druitt** You don't think I shall let you go now that I have found you.

**Marie** A trap. A trap.

**Druitt** A trap indeed, my search is at last over.

*The Lights of the Music Hall come up—we are now in a scene of melodrama*

**Marie** Let me go. Please have mercy.

**Druitt** What mercy have you ever shown, you, who have ruined everything
you ever touched?

**Marie** I am innocent, I swear I am. I swear by all that is holy, you have
the wrong girl.

**Dan** (*in the audience*) You said it!

**Marie** (*aside to Dan*) Shut your bleeding mouth, Mendoza! (*Falling into
a melodramatic pose*) Please let me go. I'll do anything.

**Druitt** Anything?

**Marie** Anything.

**Dan** Get in there, nob, it's your birthday!

**Druitt** No. My mind is made up. For years I have been searching for you.
Now that I have you in my clutches the final curtain can at last be rung
down and the play can end.

**Dan** And about bloody time, too.

**Lizzie** Shut your mouth, Mendoza!

**Dinky** Shut yours, Liz, or you'll swallow the place.

**Dan** (*hitting Dinky*) Who asked you to interfere? I apologize for my friend's behaviour. Pray continue.

**Druitt** You are in my power and here you will stay. Your cries are in vain, your pleas are in vain, your protestations are in vain . . .

**Dan** So's your bloody acting!

*A general rumpus and row breaks out*

**Chairman** I beg you. I implore you, ladies and gentlemen I remonstrate with you—a little order, PLEASE. I am fully aware that we are honoured with a passionate, sensitive, artistic and, need I add, ARTICULATE audience—but please, sit back and enjoy the scintillating performances of Whitechapel's—nay London's—nay ENGLAND's most revered thespian who has graced us with his company tonight.

*Dan blows a raspberry*

I beg your pardon, *madam*, does your husband know you're here?

**Druitt** If you can't keep quiet, sir, I shall leave. I am trying to play a dramatic scene with this lady.

**Dan** *Lady?* Her? (*He sings*)

"WHAT A LIFE"                    No. 6

Don't you know what the lady's really doing for
A living?
Is she selling something tasty on the
Corner of the street?
We can give you a little clue
By saying she's expensive
And her times are divided
Between on and off her feet
Now the trade is quite secret
So don't breathe a word to mother
It's the oldest profession
And we don't mean making sweets.

Here's another one who's at it
You can see the way she's walking
When she stops and gazes upwards
She's not looking at the night
She's waiting for the bloke behind
To get a little nearer
When he does she'll drop her handkerchief
And nod the way inside

**Boys** The trade is quite secret
So don't breathe a word to mother

It's the oldest profession
And we don't mean making jam.

What a life some of them lead
What a life
To spend the whole day charving
What a life
But on the other hand it's true
Opportunities are few
And it can't be worse than starving
What a life.

**A Man** Here, Cathy, coming up the alley, girl?

**Cathy** How much you got?

**Dan** Not enough to satisfy you, darling.

**Cathy** You keep your filthy remarks to yourself, son, or I'll get my brothers down here to do you up.

**Dan** Brothers? You don't even know who your mother was. Come along, chaps—I'll show you where you can find some real ladies.

**Girls** *Ladies!*

**Cathy** (*singing*) You wouldn't recognize a lady
    If one hit you in the face
    And don't play "Jack-the-lad"
    With me, my friend.
    Men are the cause of half the trouble
    If they'd only realize it
    I am me and I ain't changing
    So why should I pretend?

**Liza** Oh you think you're "oh so clever"
    With your fancy dandy ways
    Well don't play "Jack-the-lad"
    With me, my friend,

**All** My friend.

**Martha** 'Cos God gave me a mouth to use
    And I can bleeding use it
    So don't go starting something
    You couldn't even end.

| **Boys** What a life some of them lead | **Girls** What a life indeed |
|---|---|
| What a life | What a life |
| To spend the whole day charving | Oh what a miserable |
| What a life | Life |
| But on the other hand it's true | Oh yes, it's true |
| Opportunities are few | They're few |

**All** And it can't be worse than
    Starving, what a life.

*Music link*

**Dan** Here's another one who's fallen
    You can tell it by the patter

And she's hiding in the shadder
Out the way          **A Man** Good job too.
And the bloke'll get a shock
He hasn't seen her rotten clock
And she must be forty? six . . .
**Boys** If she's a day
Now I'm not all religious
In the true sense of the word
And I've done some naughty things
Myself, it's true.       **Girls** That's true
But here I draw the line
You wouldn't catch me selling mine
But you're welcome to my sister
If you've got a bob or two.
**Girls** Oh you!       **Boys** Yoo hoo
You're so superior      So superior
And us poor girls live
On a different plane     You're on a different plane

Oh yes!
We're so inferior
Well if that's the sort of thing     Oh yes!
You think      So inferior
You'd better think again
'Cos God gave us a pair of eyes
To see through the likes of you
So don't come "Jack-the-lad"
With me, my friend, my friend.
**Lizzie** Next time you want a favour
You can go and whistle for it
**Girls** I've got nothing more to say to you
And I hope that that's the end
**Boys** What a life some of them lead    **Girls** What a life indeed
What a life      What a life
To spend the whole day charving   Oh what a
What a life      Miserable life
But on the other hand it's true   Oh yes it's true
Opportunities are few    They're few.
**All** And it can't be worse than starving
What a life.
And it can't be worse than starving
It can't be worse than starving
It can't be worse than starving
What a l-i-f-e . . .

*The Lights fade to a Black-out, then come up on the Chairman's area,
representing the interior of Toynbee Hall, where Druitt and Marie are going
through a bundle of clothes*

**Druitt** Let me see. Yes, I'll have this one. Old? Some of these things are
in very good condition!

**Marie** That's right. I like to look after my stuff.

**Druitt** What sort of price did you have in mind?

**Marie** I dunno, as much as you could afford. I owe half a guinea to Liz
and I've got a few other expenses.

**Druitt** I couldn't manage that!

**Marie** What do you do with all this stuff, anyway?

**Druitt** We give it to those who need it most‚

**Marie** Why do you do it?

**Druitt** What?

**Marie** This job—how much do you get?

**Druitt** Nothing.

**Marie** Come off it.

**Druitt** (*laughing*) No. There are people that sometimes do something for
nothing.

**Marie** You're the first I've ever met. Why?

**Druitt** I don't know really—but we do. This dress is hardly worn. You
must have plenty of clothes to get rid of things like this.

**Marie** Yeah—I can get hold of clothes all right, that's easy.

**Druitt** But this is almost new.

**Marie** I know—but it's a bit small for me now.

**Druitt** (*holding the dress to her*) Very small in fact. It belonged to Polly—
didn't it?

**Marie** What if it did, she won't be needing it now, will she?

**Druitt** No. But it's not yours, is it?

**Marie** Well, whose is it? It's not Polly's, that's for sure and if we don't get
hold of it before the coppers—it'll never see the light of day again.

**Druitt** It's still not right!

**Marie** Not right! If you're going to worry about what's right you won't
last five minutes down here. Polly was a mate of mine and if she was
here now she'd tell you, that I could have them and welcome to 'em.
Come on—how much?

**Druitt** Four shillings?

**Marie** Right—done! You're so clever, ain't yer, I would have taken three-
and-a-tanner.

**Druitt** Well, I could have paid five shillings—so that makes us about even.

*They smile and shake hands*

(*Still holding her hand*) Marie, have you ever thought of doing something
else?

**Marie** (*pulling away*) Oh Gawd, here we go.

**Druitt** Thinking about it would be a start.

**Marie** Start of what? All the bloody lecturing and pompous preaching.
I'd have to sing an hymn or two and say me prayers, I suppose. No,
thank you—I'd rather starve, mate.

**Druitt** I'm not meaning to preach to you. I would just like to help. Per-
haps I could find you a job in service or something.

**Marie** I'm nobody's lackey. Anyway, I've got a job!

**Druitt** It's not what I call a job.

**Marie** Oh no, you wouldn't, would you? But then you don't know what's what, do you?

**Druitt** No, and I never will. As soon as anyone gets near to you people, you slam the door in their face.

**Marie** I can look after myself, mate, don't worry.

**Druitt** There are times when we all need help, Marie.

**Marie** Well I don't.

**Druitt** One of these days you will—then it might not be there.

**Marie** I'll worry about that when the time comes—meanwhile, me old Toynbee, customers are waiting.

**Druitt** For you to satisfy their lustful and indulgent desires.

**Marie** Oh—is that what you call it?

**Druitt** What would you call it?

**Marie** A little bit of loving.

**Druitt** You are not confusing that with love?

**Marie** Look, whatever you call it, however you do it, we all want it. You want it—I want it—WE ALL WANT . . . (*singing*)

"LOVE"

No.<br>7

Love.
That's what we're all looking for
Whether you're wealthy or
Whether you're poor
Once you have had it
You'll always want more

You want
I want
We all want
Love.
The singer, the music, the song
If love's not the motive
That drives us along
Then I'll admit
I'm wrong.

Both saints and sinners
Join in its praise
All walks of life
Play its game
In love there's no barrier
Colour or race
Once bitten, the smitten
Will all feel the same.

You want
I want

We all want
Love.
Of that there's no shadow of doubt
It's a free luxury
That you can't do without
That's what the whole
Rigmarole is about.

You want, I want
We all want
Love
It lightens and brightens
The day
For love is the smiling
The fighting, the crying
And that's all I'm trying to say.

The highest, the lowest
The strongest, the weak
Each gets caught up in the game
Some can't stop talking
Others can't speak
Once bitten, the smitten
Will all feel the same.

You want
I want
We all want
Love
Of that there's no shadow of doubt
The fighting, the sighing
The singing, the crying
That's what the whole
Rigmarole is about.

*The Lights fade to a Black-out. A light flashes—it is a Policeman with a bull-lamp. The Lights fade up to suggest a misty street. The Policeman sees a bundle on the street, approaches it tentatively and taps it with his foot*

**Police Sergeant** Oi, what are you doing down there? Come on, you can't sleep there. (*No movement*) Are you all right?

*Annie Chapman is the bundle, and she rises, wearing her feathered hat*

**Annie** (*tipsily*) It was only a violet, plucked for her mother's grave. Hello, sailor, how about a bit of a going over, eh?
**Police Sergeant** Now—now. Don't be saucy, you get along home.
**Annie** I'm there, ducky. This is it. Look at it, ain't it lovely? It needs a bit of tidying-up, of course. Drop in any time.
**Police Sergeant** Come on, you can't hang about the streets all night, it's against the law.

**Annie** What law? You can't turn a girl out of her home, that is against the law—I'll call a copper.

**Police Sergeant** Look, you've had enough to drink for one night.

**Annie** I ain't got nowhere to go, can I come back with you?

**Police Sergeant** I don't think the missus would understand, somehow. Be a good girl and nip round to Mitre Square. If you get done over there I won't have to write out the report.

**Annie** You couldn't spare me tuppence, could you?

**Police Sergeant** Now where do you think I'm going to get tuppence from, eh?

**Annie** If I did something wrong, would I get put in prison for the night?

**Police Sergeant** You done something wrong, have yer?

**Annie** Yeah. I pinched this hat.

**Police Sergeant** Well—you needed it, didn't you!

**Annie** What about if I broke a window?

**Police Sergeant** Now you behave yourself. We've got no room for the likes of you. Now just you be gone when I come round this way again— or there'll be trouble.

*The Police Sergeant exits*

**Annie** Just like a violet . . .

*A shadow crosses the back wall*

Who's that?

*As Annie looks towards where the shadow was, it seems to appear somewhere else on the stage, and again somewhere else. She turns from side to side, becoming terrified. At once four shadows materialize together with blood-curdling screams—it is Dan and the Boys, dressed in capes and hats. They sing*

"RIPPER'S GOING TO GET YOU"

**No. 8**

**Dan and the Boys** There you are minding your own business
When out of the shadows
Comes a big black hat
Creeps up
Eyes shut
Ssswish your bleeding throat's cut
The Ripper's going to get you if you don't
Watch out.
**Dan** Late one night you're walking down an alley
When suddenly a shriek will make your blood
Run cold
**Boys** Creeps up
Eyes shut
Ssswish your bleeding throat's cut

The Ripper's going to get you if you don't
Watch out
**Annie** Oh Gawd
What the hell was that?
**Boys** I thought I saw the Devil
In a big black hat
**Annie** Oh Gawd
**Slop** Another tart rubbed out.
**Dinky** Her tongue is slowly turning black
**Blue** Her eyes are popping out,
**Dan** She was a pretty thing before
Now she's an heap upon the floor
Look around
**Boys** Around—he's coming up behind yer
He's got a great big bloody weapon
In his hand.

Creeps up
Eyes shut
Sswish your bleeding throat's cut
The Ripper's going to get you if
You don't watch out.
**Dinky** Look out—behind you.
**Annie** You ought to be ashamed of yourself, you did. Scaring the living
daylights out of a poor girl like that. As if there isn't enough to be
frightened of around here.
**Dan** Scare the daylights out of you? Leave off. A geezer would take one
look at you and run off screaming himself. (*He sings*)
Have you heard about a bloke called
Bluebeard?
Had so many wives he had to do them in
**Annie** (*spoken*) Nice toff
Talked soft.
**Boys** He cut their bleeding heads off.
**Dan** If Bluebeard doesn't get you
Watch out for spring-heeled Jack
**Boys** Oh Lord
Was that a nasty dream.
Or did I hear another Ripper victim
Scream?
**Annie** Oh Gawd
**Slop** Is that a body there?
**Annie** Where?
**Dan** Half her insides hanging out
**Bluenose** With bloody matted hair
**Dinky** She was a fair old looking tart
Now she's been almost torn apart
**Boys** What was that—?

**Boys** —A-leaping from the shadows
With a great big bloody weapon in
His hand

Creeps up
Eyes shut
Sswish your bleeding throat's cut
The Ripper's going to get you if you
Don't watch out.

*During the last verse another cloaked figure joins the Boys and keeps in time with their movements. The Boys move off—Annie screaming after them*

*Dan and the Boys exit*

**Annie** Go on, laugh, all of you, you'll be sorry. It'll be my turn to laugh at you one of these days. Clear off! Good-bye and good-bloody-riddance! (*She turns and comes face to face with the remaining cloaked figure*) Well—what the bloody-hell do you want?

*The Figure cuts Annie's throat*

*The Lights fade to a Black-out. As they do so we hear the cry of Paper Boys in the distance*

**Paper Boys** Paper! Murder! 'Orrible murder! Paper . . . Victim . . . Murder . . . Ripper . . . Paper . . . Murder . . . Paper . . . Murder . . . Paper . . .

CURTAIN

ENTR'ACTE

# ACT II

*The crowds drift back into the Music Hall. As the Chairman enters, the Lights come up*

**Chairman** Welcome back, ladies and gentlemen, to the concluding act of tonight's thrilling performance. Are we all happy?
**All** Yes...
**A Man** But we haven't got any money to buy our beer.
**Chairman** Never mind. Charlie's going to let us have it on the slate.
**All** Hurrah...
**A Man** But no-one can pay him back.
**All** Boo...
**Chairman** Never mind. We'll be all right when the boat comes in.
**All** (*chanting*) When the boat comes in.
**Chairman** And now, ladies and gentlemen, once again I ask you to raise your glasses and drink a loyal toast to our much-beloved and kind-hearted Queen Victoria—God bless her.

"GOD BLESS" (*Reprise*)

No.
1

**All** God bless her. (*Singing*)
    God bless our Glorious Queen
    And may she reign forever more.
    A finer lady never lived
    Of this I am quite sure
    She thinks of us, she prays for us
    Good life, good luck, good health.
    And if you've any problems—
**Lizzie** —Then keep them to yourself.

*Lizzie has adopted the character of Queen Victoria. This can be done very simply, i.e. a handkerchief on top of her head—like a small veil and a shawl—the simpler the better*

    Thank you, loyal subjects. (*A raspberry*)
    And the same to you
    You're being ignored and sat on
    And this will never do
    I'll get rid of your problems
    Just leave them all to me
    Provided I can fit them
    Some time between lunch and tea
**A Man** Gawd—you're ugly!
**Lizzie** You're drunk.

**A Man** At least I'll be sober in the morning.

**Lizzie** You insulting, vulgar little man, I'll teach you a lesson. Where's Charlie?

**A Man** You called, your Majesty.

**Lizzie** Not you, Charlie. You, Charlie. My new Chief of Police Charlie.

*The Chairman puts on a hat with a cockade, the type worn by an admiral or governor-general—he is now Sir Charles Warren*

**Warren** (*singing*) You'll have noticed I've a very fine hat
   And a horse with a very fine mane
   Allow me to introduce myself
   Charles Warren is the name
   I'm the man that they push forward
   When they've got a mob to tame
   When there's been an almighty political cock-up
   And someone must take the blame.

**Victoria** Now what's this I hear about you killing people in Africa?

**Warren** Oh yes, your Majesty, twelve hundred to be exact, who will never see the light of day again.

**Victoria** Did you have a reason.

**Warren** Oh yes, they were black you know.

**Victoria** Were they revolting?

**Warren** Not arf! (*Singing*)
   I've battered the blacks in Bangaloo
   I've routed the rebels in Spain
   The wayward wogs on the Isle of Dogs
   Won't cause any trouble again
   The sleeping Sikhs in the Tin Ma Jin
   Are always on the run
   I've put liquorice in their lemon tea
   And showed them the end of me gun.

**Victoria** Yes, I hear it's a formidable weapon.

**Warren** Oh yes, your Majesty, especially in the right hands.

**Victoria** I should like to have a hold of it for a minute.

**Warren** Oh—you are a one!

**Victoria** Now bend down.

**Warren** You're all talk, you are.

**Victoria** Now give it to me.

**Warren** Is that an invitation or an exclamation?

**Victoria** (*singing*) It's a Royal Decree
   So on your knee
   Now arise, Sir Charles me boy
   You're now a knight
   So go and fight
   They need you in Sampoy.
   There's hope you might get shot there
   We'll be rid of your ugly mug
   And if you're duffed

We can have you stuffed
Or even made into a rug.
**All** And if you're duffed
We can have you stuffed
Or even made into a rug.
**Victoria** Now, now, let us get down to the serious business of the day. What is this I hear about murder in the East End?
**Warren** Oh yes, your Majesty. A politician was robbed to death on Tooting Common. A reward of ten thousand pounds has been offered.
**Victoria** *Tooting?* That isn't in the East End—is it?
**Warren** Isn't it? No wonder we couldn't find him.
**Victoria** I was referring to the other murders.
**Warren** Sir William Makepeace Thorp, strangled—five thousand pounds reward.
**Victoria** No.
**Warren** Lord Clementine Cavendish, stabbed—three thousand pounds reward?
**Victoria** No.
**Warren** The Right Honourable Sir Frederick Nightingale—done to death —two thousand pounds?
**Victoria** No—Polly Ann Nichols, the Aldgate whore!
**Warren** Oh—the fourpenny touch!
**Victoria** (*singing*) A wicked wayward bunch of girls
Who sell themselves for cash
Are being pursued by a maniac
Who gives them a right old bash
He rips the tarts to pieces
And rapes them one by one
It's got to be stopped
And I really don't see
Why they should have all the fun.
Rule Britannia
Aren't I very good
I take an interest
Like a good Queen should.
**All** Rule Britannia
Queen of all our shores
There's a rumour
That you don't wear drawers.

*The stage empties, leaving a section on stage, left or right, lit up to represent Marie's lodging*

*Druitt appears, meeting a Man*

**Druitt** Excuse me. Do you know where I might find Marie Kelly?
**A Man** Never 'eard of her.

*The Man goes. Frances Coles appears*

**Druitt** Do you know where I might find Marie Kelly?
**Frances Coles** No . . . But if I see her, who shall I say was asking for her?
**Druitt** Doesn't matter.
**Frances Coles** Nice name—Jewish?

*Frances Coles goes. Dinky appears*

**Druitt** Where does Marie Kelly live?
**Dinky** (*pointing*) Over there.
**Druitt** (*going over to Marie's lodging*) Marie. Marie, I want to speak to you.

*Marie appears. Dinky goes*

**Marie** Go away.
**Druitt** I was wondering if there were any of Annie Chapman's possessions left?
**Marie** How should I know?
**Druitt** Well, you seem to end up with the belongings of the dead.
**Marie** If there was anything left—there ain't now, unless this old hat's any good to you. (*She throws the hat at his feet*)
**Druitt** I want to talk to you.
**Marie** (*slightly drunk*) I don't feel like talking.
**Druitt** You're drunk, aren't you?
**Marie** What if I am, want to make something of it?
**Druitt** Not particularly.
**Marie** (*mocking*) Not par-tic-u-lar-ly. Go on, get out of it. You're not human, you're not. You don't drink, you don't swear, you don't even have a bit of the other. You must be dead, Druitt.
**Druitt** Not at all, but I don't have to keep talking about it.
**Marie** Bloody liar. You're dead, you are. You're a corpse come back from the dead to haunt us. Don't tell me, I know, mate. I might be ignorant, but I know about men and I know more about men than you'll ever know about women. (*She stumbles*)
**Druitt** Sit down.
**Marie** I don't want to sit down.
**Druitt** Sit down. You're cold, put this around you.
**Marie** I'm not cold.
**Druitt** Then you're frightened.
**Marie** 'Course I ain't, what do you take me for? Well, what if I am? First Polly, then Annie, who's next?
**Druitt** There won't be a next time.
**Marie** That's what they said last time.
**Druitt** They are more organized now. Something will be done.
**Marie** That's nice—you tell Polly and Annie that, they will be pleased.
**Druitt** The Queen, herself, is taking an interest.
**Marie** So's my Aunt Fanny. If I had any sense I'd be off like a shot. When Annie was done in—that was meant for me.

**Druitt** Why do you say that?

**Marie** She was wearing my hat, wasn't she?

**Druitt** Coincidence!

**Marie** Was it a coincidence that Polly Anne used to sometimes share my room and Martha Tabram looked so like me that people thought we were twins? It's me he's after!

**Druitt** Pure imagination.

**Marie** Coincidence—imagination. All right. But I'm bloody terrified.

**Druitt** Then why not go, there's nothing to keep you here, is there?

**Marie** Only me mates.

**Druitt** I meant family—relations.

**Marie** Oh—sod them.

**Druitt** Then what is stopping you? You have a choice, everybody does. I chose to live and work here—if you wish, you can choose to leave.

**Marie** It would be a waste of time—I'd only come back.

**Druitt** Why should you?

**Marie** Because they always do. My mother, her mother and her mother before her. Yes, they always talked about leaving but none of them ever did—or if they did they always came flying right back again. (*She sings*)

"HALF-A-DOZEN PINTS"    No. 2

Oh yes the grass on the other side
Is always greener
And the air down at Blackwall don't
Arf stink
Yeah I'm gonna to get away—and I really
Will tomorrow
But I'll just go down the boozer and have
Just one last drink.

Half a dozen pints
On a Friday night
And even living down this bleeding
Street's all right
When you're feeling great
And you've had a plate
Of the finest mustard pickles in the
Whole of London
It makes me creep
It's such a filthy street
And I wouldn't give you tuppence for the
Blokes you'll meet
But a few light ales
And we can all be pals
And we're all too drunk to say good-bye.

Oh the world is lovely,
Beautiful and sweet
Life's one big playground full of fun.
But by morning it's different
You're left crying on the street
And it's not all ring o' roses in the
Midday sun.

But blow your troubles, push them all away
Forget about tomorrow, that's another day
'Cos you can't go wrong
With a good sing song
And a little bit of ai-ai whoops—and
How's your father
Come on, Gladys, get your knickers down
Let's all ee-i-addio to Mother Brown
Let us sink a few
All good Cockneys do
And get so drunk that no-one gives a damn.

The breeze is lovely
Blowing from the docks
And they say a drop of sea air does you good
But when you're sober
It chokes you
It's the smell of dirty socks
And then you realize the kids have worn
Their shoes out.

The pieman's scarpered
And the chip shop's shut
We've all had an eyeful
And we're all half-cut
So the girls start crying
And it's Auld Lang Syne
And we'll all walk together arm in arm.

*The music continues*

That's what this place has always meant to me, great when you're drunk
but bloody awful when you're sober. (*She sings*)
Tho' it's nothing to be proud of
And it's not so grand
It's just a way of living here
Since time began
Tho' it's not a lot
It's all we've got
You weren't born here so you'd never understand.

*A ship's hooter is heard in the distance. They listen. It is heard again*

**A Voice in the Distance** There's a boat coming in.

*Music*

**Marie** (*singing*) There's a boat coming in.

*Music*

"THERE'S A BOAT COMING IN" **No. 3**

**A Man** There's a boat coming in
    Wake up, Harr-io
    There'll be work I know
    For anyone who wants it.
**Concerted** There's a boat coming in
    Wake up, Harr-io
    There'll be work I know
    To make the women smile
    There's a boat coming in
    Come on, Joe-io
    Wake up, Bill-io
    Get him moving
    Get there first
    Don't be slow-io
    There'll be jobs I know
    To keep you for a while.

    There's a boat coming in
    Hear the sound-io
    See the gang-io
    Shout his orders
    Work the bridge
    Let him in-io
    Take the mate below
    To the boozer
    He'll buy drink
    And pay the bill-io
    We'll sing-io
    The boat at last is in.

*The song builds up as a round. As it ends, the Chairman puts up a notice—*
*"No More Wanted"*

**Chairman** No more wanted.
**A Worker** But you only took forty on.
**Chairman** Think yourself lucky.
**A Worker** Yeah—you're all right if your face fits.
**Chairman** Well, yours don't. So that's it, mate!
**A Worker** Any more heading this way?
**Chairman** How should I know, I'm not the bloody oracle. (*He sings un-accompanied*)

## "THERE AIN'T ANY WORK TODAY"

There ain't any work today
I don't care what the other dockers say
There ain't any work today

They ain't taking on any more
I don't care what you heard before
They ain't taking on any more

There's a way of looking at it
If you'd see their point of view
It calls at all the other docks
Takes on a hand or two
By the time it's got to Limehouse Reach
The ship's got all it's crew
So there ain't any work today

**Crowd** Oh, Gawd blimey
When's the next one due?

**Chairman** (*speaking*) How should I know—I'm not the bloody oracle!

**Crowd** (*singing*) Oh, Gawd blimey
What are we to do?

**Chairman** There's no use in getting stroppy
We know that times are thin
You could be a long time waiting
So you'd better turn it in
One day an empty ship will come
And there'll be work again
But there ain't any work today.

*The people all sit dejected in the street—staring straight ahead. There is a solitary stillness*

*Dinky and Dan enter*

**Dinky** Dan, here.

**Dan** What d'you want?

**Dinky** I've got something to tell you.

**Dan** What?

**Dinky** You know that geezer from Toynbee Hall?

**Dan** Yeah!

**Dinky** You know Long Lizzie's place?

**Dan** Yeah.

**Dinky** You know Marie?

**Dan** 'Course I bloody do. What are you on about?

**Dinky** Well—I saw both of them.

**Dan** That's nice for you. Christ, you're a nit.

**Dinky** No, Dan, they were together, all close and that.

**Dan** So? He probably had his hand up her skirt or maybe he was giving
her one—what's wrong with that?

**Dinky** No, Dan, it was worse than that. They were talking.

**Dan** (*shocked*) *Talking?* This is bloody serious, Dinky, ol' son.

**Dinky** Yeah, Liz was at the door having an ear-wig and I was having a gander through the back window. She was on about leaving—going away and that.

**Dan** In'it marvellous, eh? You get a tart all nice and ignorant, like putty in your hands and along comes some educated, toffee-nosed ponce—full of clever ideas—and where are you?

**Dinky** Dunno, Dan.

**Dan** You end up *working* for a living.

**Dinky** *Working?* Oh no. I'll go down and slip him a crippler.

**Dan** No, Dinky, my ol' son. I've got a better idea—round up the boys, I'll see you down the Steampacket.

**Dinky** (*looking at the silent people*) Look at her.

**Dan** Look at him.

**Dinky** Bloody waxworks!

*Dinky and Dan exit*

*The people sing*

"LOOK AT THEM"   No.
                 5

**First Man** Look at her
    Counts her money out
    Putting each penny in a tin.
    Tells the street
    Can't make two ends meet
    Then spends it all on gin.

**Second Man** That old girl
    All of eighty-eight
    Look at her heaving sacks of coal
    No-one left
    Not a single soul
    She drove them up the pole.

**First Woman** See him there
    Sleepin' in the chair
    My old man in the checkered coat
    One dark night
    When it's nice and quiet
    I'll cut his bleeding throat.

**All** (*speaking*) Hark at her!

**Men** (*singing*) Is life worse than
    A nagging wife
    On and on
    Till you're dead and gone
    One dark night
    When I'm good and tight
    I'll cut her bleeding throat.

**All** Look at them
On the other side
Sitting there
With a lardy-air
Take charity
That's a certainty
Where the hell's their pride?

Neighbourly
All in harmony
Such a friendly close-knit family
Man to man
Do the best you can
And together we will stand

Don't you tell us
We've heard it all before
Too many promises are broken
Too many times
Too many lies before
Our eyes are open.

*The people exit silently*

*Dan, Bluenose, Slop and Dinky gather at the Steampacket*

**Bluenose** What's your idea, Dan?
**Dan** We're going to get Druitt once and for all.
**Slop** Right, Dan, I'll go down and give him one.
**Dan** Slop, my ol' son.
**Slop** Yes?
**Dan** Shut up. It's no good doing him up—he'd love all that.
**Dinky** What's your idea then?
**Dan** We'll fix him up good and proper—and I think I know how—like bang—we'll get him nicked.
**Dinky** Drop him in the shit, eh?
**Dan** Beautifully put, my ol' son, I couldn't have said it better meself.
**Slop** But how, Dan? He's a clever old geezer.
**Dan** We'll get him picked up for all these murders. Write a letter incriminating him.
**Bluenose** Great idea, Dan.
**Dinky** Yeah, but there's one snag in it.
**Slop** What's that?
**Dinky** None of us can write.
**Dan** Trust you to put the mockers on it.
**Dinky** It's an important point, Dan!
**Dan** It's only a detail though, in'it? Anyway, I've already thought of that, meet my bright friend—yours truly, Lord Overcoat.

*Lord Overcoat, the old trampish barrow boy, joins them*

There you are, that's what education can do for you. What a fine specimen of learning we have here.

**Overcoat** Piss off!

**Dan** Yes, looks like rain. I never thought I'd see the day when you'd be useful, old 'un, but this will give hundreds new hope—give the old geezer a chair—sit down, your lordship.

**Overcoat** What's it worth?

**Dan** Bluenose, get a jug of Burton for his lordship.

**Bluenose** I ain't got any money, Dan.

**Dan** That needn't stop you. Use a bit of common—nick a jug.

*Bluenose exits*

**Overcoat** Got a fag?

**Dan** (*clicking his fingers*) Slop, a fag for his lordship.

**Slop** I ain't got any, Dan.

**Dan** Find a few dog-ends and roll 'em up in a bit of newspaper. Do I have to do all the thinking round here? Right, pencil—paper. Put this down . . .

*Bluenose enters with a tray on which are a cigarette, a mug of beer and a small bowl of "blood"*

**Overcoat** What language do you want it in?

**Dan** What you got?

*Bluenose puts the tray on the table*

**Dan** Mix it up a bit, I don't mind. Put this down. "Dear Charlie . . .".

**Slop** Who's the Charlie?

**Dan** You are, you soppy bugger—Charlie Warren's in charge of all the investigating.

**Dinky** He's *Sir* Charles Warren, isn't he?

**Dan** So—what if he is?

**Dinky** You have to address him as your lordship, his excellency or maybe —your honour.

**Dan** You've been in front of too many judges, Dinky my old son.

**Overcoat** Hurry, can't you, I've got to get back to me barrow.

**Dan** Right—put this down. "Dear—Guv'nor. Beware, I shall soon be back at work again, I am down on all whores and I won't stop . . ."

**Overcoat** (*writing*) Wait a minute. ". . . whores—won't stop . . ."

**Dan** "Until I get buckled." Now to drop Toynbee in it . . .

**Overcoat** ". . . drop Toynbee in it . . ."

**Dan** No, not you, you soppy sod. Scrub it out, just put down what I tell you.

**Dinky** You could drop Toynbee in it, by saying "I work at Toynbee Hall".

**Dan** No—too obvious—you got to be subtle.

**Bluenose** What's that?
**Dan** Bloody sly.
**Dinky** What about—"I'm right under your nose"?

*Dan sniffs Lord Overcoat and moves away*

**Dan** Dinky, you're a genius. Well, put that down.
**Overcoat** What?
**Dan** "You'll never get me, 'cos I'm right under your nose."
**Slop** "I'm a friend of all whores."
**Boys** Yeah, that's good, Slop—great!
**Slop** (*taking over*) "Friend of all whores—and everyone—knows."
**Dinky** Here, that rhymes.
**Dan** What does?
**Dinky** That. "You'll never catch me. I'm under your nose. I'm a friend of all whores that everyone knows."

*The Boys, except Dan, begin to chant the rhyme and move about to it*

**Dan** (*stopping them*) You wouldn't like to get up on the stage and do a little dance as well, would you? You've all gone potty. Right—where were we?
**Overcoat** We just dropped Toynbee in it.
**Dan** Put this down. "I'll give you a tip. The next time I rip. An whore from ear to ear. It will be in——"
**Dinky** '—Mitre Squeer." (*He means "square"*)

*The other boys clap and laugh*

**Dan** (*very put out*) I was going to say that—write your own bloody letter. Aw go on—read it back.
**Overcoat** I can't.
**Dan** You can't? Are you taking the piss?
**Overcoat** I can't, that's the truth!
**Dan** You've just written the letter. How can you do that if you can't read?
**Overcoat** Simple—I broke me glasses.

*The Chairman enters*

**Dan** Gawd help the lot of us. (*He turns to the Chairman*) Oi, mate, can you read?
**Chairman** (*reading*) "Beware, I shall soon be back at work again. I am down on all whores, and I won't stop until I get buckled." (*He gives Dan a strange look*) "You'll never find me 'cos I'm right under your nose. I'm a friend of all whores, that everyone knows. I'll give you a tip. The next time I rip an whore from ear to ear it will be in Mitre Square." (*He gives Dan a long look*)
**Dan** It's all right, mate, it's a letter to me girl-friend. (*To the Boys*) How about that?

*The Chairman exits*

**Dinky** Great, Dan. What about signing it?
**Dan** Yeah, we'll have to think up a good name.
**Bluenose** How about Fred the Knife?
**Dan** No—not blood-thirsty enough.
**Dinky** Slash the Knife?
**Bluenose** The Deadly Slasher from Flower and Dean Street.
**Dan** That's nearly as long as the bloody letter itself.
**Dinky** Something short and simple!
**Bluenose** Slash the Ripper.
**Slop** Rip the Slasher.
**Dinky** Jack the Slasher.
**Bluenose** Jack the Ripper.

*The Boys look at one another and think*

**Boys** JACK THE RIPPER . . .
**Dan** (*after a long pause*) No—it'll never catch on.
**Dinky** What then, Dan?
**Dan** Go on, then, Jack the Ripper will do. Now—where can we get some red ink?
**Slop** How about signing it in blood?
**Dan** Good idea—who's going to give us some blood?
**Overcoat** I can't. I ain't got any on me.
**Dan** Any volunteers?
**Bluenose** ⎤   Sod off!
**Dinky**   ⎬   Not bleeding likely!   ⎬ (*Speaking together*)
**Slop**   ⎦   Not me!
**Dan** (*to Slop*) Come on, it was your idea.
**Slop** I gave the idea—somebody else gives the blood.
**Dan** Right. We'll do this fairly—all those in favour of Slop giving the blood say "aye".
**All** (*raising hands*) Aye!
**Slop** I hate the sight of blood.
**Dan** Close your eyes, then.

*There is a struggle as the Boys grab Slop, during which Dan's finger is cut—he uses the stage blood planted on the table*

(*Half crying*) You silly sods. Now look what you've gone and done—(*pointing his bloody finger at Slop*)—I'll kill you for this.
**Dinky** We might as well use yours now, Dan.
**Dan** (*splashing blood on the letter*) A work of art—if I say so meself. Here we are. (*He scrawls an X in blood*)

*A Paper Boy rushes on, shouting very clearly*

**Paper Boy** Ripper caught—Suspect arrested—Read all about it! Ripper caught—Suspect arrested—Read all about it!

*The Music Hall comes to life, and the Lights come up on it*

*The Chairman, representing another face of authority, enters wearing a judge's wig*

**Chairman** Call the first suspect forward, please. Ladies and gentlemen, your friend and mine, number sixteen on your hymn sheets: "The Mad Butcher from Mile End—Alexander Pedachenko".

*We see this next song as a pastiche on "If I Were Not An Actor On The Stage". Each verse is done with suitable actions*

"SUSPECTS"

No.
6

**Dan** *(as a butcher; singing)* I'm known as Leather Apron
And my shop's in Berner Street
I'm known as Leather Apron
And I sell high-class meat
You can hear me all day long
A-singing of this song
I cut pigs' feet, liver and meat
I'm handy with me knife

*Action*

**All** He cuts pigs' feet, liver and meat
He's handy with his knife.

*Dan dances to the side of the stage*

**Chairman** For our next suspect, that lion—serio—comic of the Steam-packet, late Coal Hole, Mr Fogelma, the singing Norwegian Sailor.
**Dinky** *(as a sailor; singing)* I am a foreign skipper
Working boats across the sea
I am a foreign skipper
Working boats across the sea
Though I don't know why I'm here
I'm glad I could appear
I'm a skipper on a clipper
But to say I'm Jack the Ripper
Is a piece of idiocy.

*Action*

**All** He's a skipper on a clipper
But to say he's Jack the Ripper
Is a piece of idiocy.

*Dinky joins Dan at the side of the stage*

**Chairman** And now, that comic-vocalist with a wit so sharp he'll cut himself one day. Your friend and mine, Siddy Allslop.
**Slop** *(as a barber; singing)* I am a demon barber

And I live in Fleet Street
With razor, brush and lather
I'd give you quite a treat
I'd sit you in my chair
But I wouldn't cut your hair
I'd cut your throat——
**Dan** —You soppy sod
You've got it wrong—that's Sweeney Todd.
**All** He's all mixed up, he's such a dick
He's got the wrong end of the stick.

*Slop joins other two, doing their own actions*

**Chairman** By way of a pleasant diversion, that peripatetic Cockney sparrow—Miss Saucy Rosebud.
**Martha** (*singing*) They're so confused they're in a whirl
They say the Ripper is a girl
They're so confused they're in a whirl
They say the Ripper is a girl
And now they're trying to say
I put those whores away
That I'm the killer don't be daft
"Jill the Ripper", that's a laugh
**All** That she's the Ripper don't be daft
"Jill the Ripper" that's a laugh.

*Liza Pearl joins the others all doing their own actions*

**Chairman** We are now proud and privileged to present for your further enjoyment and education—the very Regal and Right Royal—Albert—Duke of Clarence . . .
**Bluenose** (*as the Duke; singing*) I'm a nob from royalty
And a high up nob I am
I'm a nob from royalty
And a high up nob I am
I'm very high and I'm very grand
You see I've an orb and thing in me hand
My robes are made from ermine
The rest is made from lace
But royalty in custody's
A dastardly disgrace.
**Lizzie** (*interrupting as Queen Victoria*) How dare you treat my grandson in this manner—he's one of us.
**A Man** You could have fooled me, I thought he was one of them.
**Victoria** Be quiet, you wretched little man, or I'll have you beheaded. Where's my Chief of Police?
**Chairman** (*changing to a hat with a cockade*) Your friend and mine—Charlie Warren. (*He kneels*)
**Victoria** All right, get off your knees. Now what are you going to do about these Whitechapel murders?

**Warren** Ignore them and they might go away.
**Victoria** Have you checked out all the single men living in rooms in that
    part of London?
**Warren** No.
**Victoria** Have you traced all the lunatics that have escaped from asylums?
**Warren** No.
**Victoria** Have you issued the poor unfortunates with police whistles?
**Warren** No.
**Victoria** Have the police dressed up as women?
**Warren** Eh?
**Victoria** In the hope of being accosted by the beast.
**Warren** No.
**Victoria** Have bloodhounds been set loose to track the killer?
**Warren** *Yes*, your Majesty.
**Victoria** Oh, good. What happened?
**Warren** We lost them.

*There is a groan from the crowd*

    Well, it was foggy.
**Victoria** (*singing*) Oh, Charlie lad, it's very bad
        So off to Aldgate East
        And, Charlie lad, although you're mad
        Do try and keep the peace
**Warren** But no-one will co-operate
        I drive them round the bend
        For I'm the man that they most hate
**Victoria** And the obvious man to send

        A message to my subjects
        Good life, good luck, good health
        And if you're wanting something done
        Then do it your bleeding self

        Rule Britannia
        Aren't I very good
        I take an interest
        Like a good Queen should
**All** Rule Britannia
        Queen of England's shores
        She's the saviour
        Who will save our whores.

*A patriotic tableau is struck, with the Queen in the centre like Britannia,
and the crowd draped around her. A map of the area is lit up*

**Druitt** Right. Group one; patrol a square bordered by Middlesex Street
    to the west; Mile End Waste to the east; Whitechapel Road going north
    to Hanbury Street. Group two: Whitechapel Road down to Cable
    Street; bordered by the Minories to the west and Watney Street to the
    east. Group three; I want you to patrol the alleys and lanes around

Spitafields and Itchy Park. If you see anything at all suspicious—blow your whistles.

*The crowd exits, blowing whistles and carrying bull-lamps*

*The Lights fade to a dim stage*

*A face appears round a corner, then a Sergeant of Police gingerly steps forward wearing a bonnet and apron dress over his uniform. He is obviously a policeman, taking Victoria's suggestions to heart*

"POLICEMAN'S CHORUS"         No.
                                             7

**Sergeant** (*singing*) Yerse—they've gone and dressed me up
    In women's clothes
    And it's not the sort of job I would
    Have chose
    I understood the pay was good
    The prospects not too bad
    The pension scheme's encouraging
    But still I'm feeling sad
    They took away my little truncheon
    And gave me a little bag . . .

*Three more Policemen join the Sergeant—dressed similarly: the bigger and tougher they look the more effective this number*

**All**  And they've gone and dressed us up
    In women's clothes.
    Yes, they've gone and dressed us up
    In women's clothes
    And it's not the sort of job I would
    Have chose
**First Policeman** The station sergeant looks all right
    If a trifle fat
**Second Policeman** Inspector Horn's a nice old tart
    But just a little flat
**Third Policeman** And Charlie's putting knickers on
    And no-one said do that
**All** Oh my Gawd . . .
    And he's sewing on a lot of
    Frilly bows
**Sergeant** Mind you, I wouldn't like to say a lot
    But Albert's quite enjoying it
    He's putting rouge and make-up on
    And mincing up and down a bit
    He's been propositioned three times
    And he hasn't turned them down yet

**All** And he's gone and got dressed up in
Women's clothes.
**First Policeman** When I was told to dress like
Some old whore—
**All** Some old whore
**First Policeman** I thought "funny"
Never heard of that before—
**All** Never heard of that before
**Second Policeman** It's not the sort of job that I would
Normally revere
**Third Policeman** Now I'll tell you something
You'll be surprised to hear
**Sergeant** Fourteen hundred coppers
Couldn't wait to volunteer
**All** When the cry went up "get dressed"
When the cry went up "get dressed"
When the cry went up "get dressed"
In women's clothes . . .

*The Police march off smartly*

*A Light comes up at Long Lizzie's*

*Marie is seen to be creeping away*

**Lizzie** Oi, hello, Marie dear, not leaving without saying good-bye, are
you?
**Marie** Why don't you mind your own business!
**Lizzie** Now, now, that's no way to talk to an old friend. Besides, it is
my business, seeing as you owe me half-a-guinea.
**Marie** I've left me silver frame and me pink necklace, pawn them and
you'll get more than your half-a-guinea. Satisfied?
**Lizzie** All right, girl, if you say so.
**Marie** Don't you ever sleep, Liz? It must be four o'clock in the morning.
**Lizzie** Can't afford to sleep in my game, dear, not if you want to get on.
**Marie** Get on? You'd better hurry up, hadn't you?
**Lizzie** Going somewhere special, are you?
**Marie** Wouldn't you like to know, eh? But I ain't telling you, that's a
certainty, tell Long Liz and you tell the bleeding world.
**Lizzie** Not me, dear, my lips are sealed. If I told you half the things I've
heard you'd never believe me.
**Marie** I don't anyway.
**Lizzie** All right—where shall I say you've gone?
**Marie** Say you don't know—then you'll be telling the truth, for a change.
**Lizzie** Well, ta ta, girl, be seeing you then.
**Marie** On no, you won't.
**Lizzie** You'll be back—they always do.

### "STEP ACROSS THE RIVER"

**Marie** No, Liz, not this time . . . (*Singing*)
    I only have to step across the river
    It's a step that's not so very hard to make
    Yes, it only takes a step a day
    To be a million miles away
    For each little step I take
    Must lead to others

    It only takes one tiny little flower
    To make the most artistic sweet bouquet
    Yes, if you're prepared to dig away
    It only takes a spoon a day
    For you to dig the flaming world away
    You feel that life has left you way
    Behind it
    And every old ambition's dead and gone
    If only some small hope remained
    For you to stop and start again

    You'd do a lot of things you've left undone
    No, it's not too late to start a little fire

    It only needs one tiny little flame
    Yes, it only takes a spark at first
    To set alight the universe
    And every big event must start that way.

*The music continues underneath the dialogue*

**Lizzie** Maybe you're right, dear.
**Marie** I know I'm right, Liz. At least that's something I learnt from
Toynbee. I'll give him his due, you can't sit around moaning forever.
You've got to get up and do something about it. And that's what I
intend to do.
**Lizzie** Yeah, so will I, dear, sometime.
**Marie** No. *Now*, Liz.
**Lizzie** I couldn't, dear, not with all my business commitments. (*She sings*)
    I might have been a lady or a princess
    I might have lived a life of luxury
    But my life rolled on a different way
    And this is where I am today
    Fate took a hand
    And it was not to be
    You might make out a case for never trying
    Or never really wanting things to change
    Or that I let opportunity
    And chances slip away from me

**Marie** But it's as plain as plain could be
    It's easier than ABC
**Both** It only takes one tiny little flower
    To make the most artistic sweet bouquet
    Yes, if you're prepared to dig away
    It only takes a spoon a day
    For you to dig the flaming world away
    You feel that life has left you way behind it
    And every old ambition's dead and gone
    If only some small hope remained
    For you to stop and start again
    You'd do a lot of things you've left undone
    Well, it's not too late to start a little fire
    It only needs one tiny little flame
    Yes, it only takes a spark at first
    To set alight the universe
    And every big event must start that way.

*Marie exits, and Lizzie goes inside*

*The Light becomes eerie, as does the music. The stage is empty*

*Druitt enters, dressed in flowing cloak, hat, etc.*

### "MONTAGE"

No.
9

**Druitt** (*singing*) Eight little whores
    With no hope of Heaven
    Gladstone may save one
    Then there'll be seven

    Seven little whores
    Begging for a shilling
    One lives in Henage Court
    Then there's a killing.

*Music*

*The crowds rush on. The chase for the Ripper has started*

    There he goes
**All** There he goes
**Druitt** I thought I saw him
    This way
**All** Which way?
**The Boys** Running up the alley
    In a big black hat.
**All** Black hat.

**The Boys** This way.
**All** This way.
**The Boys** That way.
**All** That way
　　　Every blooming
　　　Which way
　　　Ripper's going to get you
　　　If you don't watch out!
　　　Watch out!

*The crowd rushes off in pursuit*

**Druitt** Six little whores
　　　Glad to be alive
　　　One sidles up to Jack
　　　Then there are five.

*Druitt merges with the shadows*

*A Child (Polly) enters, playing hopscotch*

**Child** Jack the Ripper stole a kipper
　　　Hid it in his father's slipper
　　　When his father put it on
　　　Jack and kipper both had gone.

*The crowd rushes on*

**First Man** There he is.
**All** There he is.
**First Man** Standing in the doorway.
**All** Doorway.
**Second Man** No he's not. He's over
　　　There at Number Four.
**All** Number Four.
**First Woman** Short bloke.
**All** Oh?
**Third Man** Tall chap.
**All** Oh!
**Second Woman** Cloth cap.
**All** Ah!
**Fourth Man** Humpty back.
**All** Oo!

　　　Ripper's going to get you
　　　If you don't watch out!
　　　Watch out! Watch out!

There—he goes . . . there he goes . . . there he goes

**Dinky** I thought that it was Toynbee
    Ripping up the tarts
    Along the Mile End waste
**All** Mile End waste
**Bluenose** Right toff!
**Slop** Leave off.
**Dan** Cut your bleeding ears off
**All** Cut your bleeding ears off

    Ripper's going to get you if
    You don't watch out!
    Watch out!

*The crowd rushes off in pursuit*

**Druitt** Four and whore rhyme aright
    So do three and me
    I'm going to set the town alight
    And have a bloody spree.

*The crowd marches on, Warren, Queen Victoria, Lizzie, and all*

**Warren** Some say that he's a doctor
    And some that he's a well-off.
**All** A well-off.
**Warren** Some say that he's a surgeon
**All** Yeah!
**Warren** And some that he's well off.
**All** Well off.
**Victoria** He cannot be an Englishman
    Of that you can be sure
**All** Hooray!
**Victoria** No Briton could be guilty
    Of such flagrance of the law.

*The Ripper creeps up and cuts Lizzie's throat. She is carried off to the*
*"Death March"*

**Warren** He cannot be an Englishman
    Of this we can be sure
**All** Be sure
**Warren** No Briton would be guilty
    Of such flagrance of the law.
**All** Right!

    The English are so honest
    Respectable and pure
    He can only be a foreigner
    Of that we can be . . .

**Paper Boy** Double murder! Two more cut from ear to ear. Double murder! 'Orrible murder! Ripper murder!

*The crowd clears from the stage*

**Druitt** (*singing*) Two little whores shivering with fright
    Seek a cosy doorway in the middle of the night
    Jack's knife flashes—then there's but one
    And the last one's the ripest for Jack's idea
    Of fun!

*Screams and panic. The crowd disperses to audience positions in the Music Hall, which is without light. Druitt and Marie come face to face*

**Marie** Look out, you bloody fool—Toynbee, you scared the living daylights out of me.
**Druitt** There's no need to be frightened any more.
**Marie** Yes. Anyway, I'm glad I got to see you before I go. We didn't always see eye to eye, you always wanting to make a stand and me always ready to earn a nimble shilling.
**Druitt** It's all over now. There's just one final scene to perform then the curtains can fall forever.

*About this time we realize that Druitt is playing out a scene from melodrama while Marie remains "real". The Music Hall lights gradually return*

**Marie** I'm leaving, Toynbee, I'm glad I had a chance to say good-bye.
**Druitt** You are all the same. You would say anything—except your prayers.
**Marie** You're not going to start anything, are you? Or I'll give you a bleeding clump.
**Druitt** I know your crimes. Your guilt. Now you must receive the punishment.
**Marie** Don't start giving me all that!
**Druitt** When the evil is cut out of a beautiful thing—only the beauty remains.
**Marie** What are you talking about?
**Druitt** You are the one I have been searching for. Only fleeting shadows have existed before you, now that I have found you, you shall never be free.
**Marie** What's the matter with you?
**Druitt** For years I have waited for revenge. Now it is within my grasp you shall not escape me—never.
**Marie** Oh my God!
**Druitt** Your mind is corrupt. Your body diseased. You shall not destroy me as you have destroyed others before me.
**Marie** Help, please, help me—someone!
**Druitt** You are in my power. Your cries are in vain, your pleas are in vain, your protestations are in vain.

*The stage audience now participate, with sounds of pleasure at her predicament—egging the villain on in quiet undertones*

**Marie** (*directly to the "melodrama" audience*) Help me, one of you, can't you? It's not a game. *Can't you see he means it?*
**Druitt** Heaven alone can help you now, Marie.
**Marie** (*to the empty Chairman's seat*) Mr Chairman! Where are you, now that I need you to stop this?
**Druitt** The body and the flesh are disposable, only the spirit and the soul are bestowed to live on forever. Come into my warm and open arms. Come. (*He takes Marie and is about to kill her*)

*The Boys arrive, also the Police Sergeant. They too are part of the "melodrama"*

**Bluenose** So! Caught in the very act, you swine.
**Dan** I have a letter here that says you are Spring-heeled Jack, the phantom killer of Petticoat Lane. What have you to say?
**Druitt** Yes. I confess. It was me.
**Dan** Villain!
**Slop** Blackguard!!
**Dinky** Scoundrel!
**Police Sergeant** I arrest you for the murders of these poor unfortunates. Come with me!
**Druitt** *Never!* NEVER! You shall never take me. Never-Never-Never.

*The Boys and Police Sergeant surround the villain. In the confusion and swirling of his cape the villain goes and the Chairman replaces him*

**Chairman** And so, ladies and gentlemen, ends another thrilling Saturday night's entertainment at the Steampacket. Your patronage is appreciated by the artists and, of course, my goodself. And now Charlie has to reluctantly close for the night. So I bid you farewell . . . but, as you wander home through the labyrinth of alleys and passageways—BEWARE—for the phantom killer lives yet. Good night.

*The last song is sung by the Company—a gentle reprise of "Saturday Night". All vestiges of the Music Hall slowly disappear, and we are left with a "real" street. During the song, audible farewells are exchanged*

"SATURDAY NIGHT" (*Reprise*)      **No. 10**

**All** Oh goodnight
Saturday night
You'll never know how I'll miss yer
When you're near
Clouds disappear
I long all week to kiss yer.

Of one thing I am quite sure
You are mine forever more
I'm the only one knows how to handle yer.

Others may come and go
No more affection could I show
Than say that no-one else
Can hold a candle to yer.

Oh goodnight (sweet)
Saturday night (sweet)
I'll dream of you please believe me.

While we're apart (safe)
Here in my heart (safe)
You'll never really leave me.

*As the music continues underneath, the final scene takes on the same shape as the opening scene. Characters are in the same positions—the dialogue is very much the same*

**Annie** 'Ere, Liz, save us a room for later.
**Lizzie** You get your fourpence, girl, I'll fix you up.
**Marie** Have you finished with my hat, Annie?
**Annie** Not yet, luv, give us a chance.
**Marie** You break the feather—I'll break your bleeding neck. (*Seeing Druitt*) Here, Polly, who's that?
**Polly** That's the psalm-singing do-gooder, Mr Druitt from Toynbee Hall.

*The others slowly drift off, leaving Marie and Druitt alone*

**Marie** Oi, oi, Toynbee, put your Bible down, son, and get hold of this. I'll give you something to sing about.
**Druitt** All right, come on then. There's no point in wasting such a fine night, just talking.
**Marie** Have you got the readys?
**Druitt** Will this do?
**Marie** No beating about the bush with your sort, is there? Come on, up this alley.
**Druitt** No, we'll go this way, it's quieter by the canal.

*Marie and Druitt exit to the "Ripper" theme and the Shadow looming on the back wall*

CURTAIN

FINALE

# FURNITURE AND PROPERTY LIST

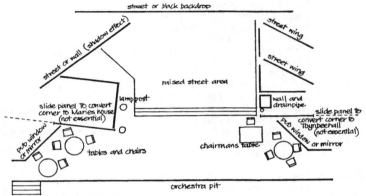

company can use stairs to sit music-hall
where available. Also orchestra pit can
be built over to accommodate tables and
chairs to link play with audience where
possible

## ACT I

*On stage:* 3 pub tables. *On them:* glasses
9 small chairs
**Chairman**'s table. *On it:* gavel
**Chairman**'s chair
Street lamp

*Off stage:* Pram with vegetables **(Lord Overcoat)**
Religious banner **(Banner Man)**
Magic cabinet and tricks **(Druitt)**
Feathered hat **(Marie)**
Broken replica of hat **(Annie)**
Suitcase with clothes **(Marie)**
Bottle **(Annie)**
4 black cloaks and hats **(The Boys)**
Knife **(Druitt)**
Bull lamp **(Policeman)**
Newspapers **(Paper Boy)**

*Personal:* **Druitt:** Bible; four shillings and sixpence
**Annie:** bag with four pennies

## ACT II

*Set:*       *On Chairman's table:* **Sir Charles's** hat, stick for sword, paper and
            pencil
            Check tables for glasses in pub

*Off stage:* Paper and pencil **(Dan)**
            Notice—NO MORE WORK TODAY **(Chairman)**
            Leather apron **(Dan)**
            Pantomime meat chopper **(Dan)**
            Pantomime telescope **(Dinky)**
            Pantomime razor **(Bluenose)**
            Cucumber and mug of beer (as orb and sceptre) **(Slop)**
            Cloak and crown **(Slop)**
            List **(Druitt)**
            Bull lamps and whistles **(Police)**
            Aprons, bags and hats **(Police Chorus)**
            Newspapers **(Paper Boy)**
            Old tin and coins **(Old Lady)**
            Tray with mug of beer, cigarette, small bowl of blood for signing
            letter **(Bluenose)**
            Suitcase **(Marie)**

*Personal:*  **Lizzie:** piece of lace for Queen's hat
            **Marie:** broken hat
            **Druitt:** sixpence

# LIGHTING PLOT

Property fittings required: street lamp, wall shadow effect
Multiple set

**ACT I.** Night

*To open:*    Effect of misty alleyways and "real street", street lamp on, Ripper shadow on wall

| | | |
|---|---|---|
| *Cue 1* | **Polly** sings "Saturday Night" song<br>*Brighten general lighting, but retain "real street" effect* | (Page 2) |
| *Cue 2* | **Marie:** ". . . filthy son of a double-eyed . . ."<br>*Snap on Music Hall lights, take out "real street". As this is the first time this "trick" is played on the Audience the effect should be positive. For the first time all the coloured lights of the Music Hall are snapped on— coloured bulbs around the proscenium, lamps scattered about the tables. If possible, a huge lit sign "STEAM PACKET MUSIC HALL" should light up; and all realistic lighting should change for stage lighting with* **Marie** *caught in a coloured spot* | (Page 7) |
| *Cue 3* | **Chairman** starts speech to Audience<br>*Bring up spot on* **Chairman**, *retain till start of song "God Bless Us"* | (Page 7) |
| *Cue 4* | At end of "God Bless Us" scene<br>*Return to "real street" lighting and Ripper shadow* | (Page 10) |
| *Cue 5* | Ripper turns into magician<br>*Return to full Music Hall lighting* | (Page 10) |
| *Cue 6* | **Chairman** starts monologue<br>*Isolate* **Chairman** *in spot. At end of monologue return to "real street" lighting* | (Page 11) |
| *Cue 7* | **Lizzie** sings "Good-bye Day" song<br>*Slow cross-fade to warm evening lighting* | (Page 12) |
| *Cue 8* | At end of "Good-bye Day" song<br>*Fade back to "real street": as* **Marie** *and* **Druitt** *turn the scene into stage melodrama fade into full Music Hall lighting* | (Page 13) |
| *Cue 9* | At end of "Jack-the-Lad" song<br>*Fade to Black-out, then come up on* **Chairman**'s *area representing Toynbee Hall* | (Page 17) |
| *Cue 10* | At end of "Love" song<br>*Fade to Black-out, then up to misty "real street" lighting* | (Page 20) |
| *Cue 11* | **Annie:** "Just like a violet . . ."<br>*Ripper shadow effect* | (Page 21) |

| | | |
|---|---|---|
| *Cue* 12 | **Boys** start "Ripper's Going to Get You" song<br>*Bring up lighting down* c *for song* | (Page 21) |
| *Cue* 13 | **Dan** and **Boys** exit<br>*Fade to spot for murder, then to Black-out* | (Page 23) |

## ACT II

*To open:* Full Music Hall lighting

| | | |
|---|---|---|
| *Cue* 14 | On general exit at end of "Rule Britannia" song<br>*Cross-fade to "real street" lighting* | (Page 26) |
| *Cue* 15 | **Dinky:** "Over there . . ."<br>*Bring up spot on* **Marie's** *room area* | (Page 27) |
| *Cue* 16 | At start of "There's a Boat" song<br>*Cross-fade to cold morning light on docks* | (Page 30) |
| *Cue* 17 | On general exit at end of "Look at Them" song<br>*Fade to spot on central area* | (Page 33) |
| *Cue* 18 | **Paper Boy** calls news<br>*Snap on full Music Hall lighting* | (Page 36) |
| *Cue* 19 | **Druitt:** ". . . blow your whistles."<br>*Fade to dim "real street" lighting* | (Page 40) |
| *Cue* 20 | **Police** exit<br>*Bring up spot on* "**Lizzie's** *house*" | (Page 41) |
| *Cue* 21 | **Marie** and **Lizzie** exit<br>*Cross-fade to eerie light effect* | (Page 43) |
| *Cue* 22 | **Druitt:** ". . . the curtains can fall for ever"<br>*Slow return to full Music Hall lighting* | (Page 46) |
| *Cue* 23 | During "Saturday Night" reprise<br>*Cross-fade to opening Act I lighting* | (Page 47) |

# EFFECTS PLOT

## ACT I

*No cues*


## ACT II

*Cue* 1    **Marie** (*singing*): "So you'd never understand"                    (Page 29)
          *Ship's hooter sounds twice in distance*

MADE AND PRINTED IN GREAT BRITAIN BY
LATIMER TREND & COMPANY LTD PLYMOUTH

MADE IN ENGLAND